AN ISAIAH FAIRY TALE

in Coordination with the Revelation of John

THE ISAIAH INSTITUTE

Illustrated by Jo Ellen Scott

Hebraeus Press

An Isaiah Fairy Tale

www.IsaiahExplained.com
www.IsaiahProphecy.com

Published in the United States of America
First Printing, 2024

Softcover ISBN 978-0-910511-62-9
E-Book ISBN 978-0-910511-63-6

Isaiah was a prophet who saw what will happen before Jesus comes again. His words are like a fairy tale. Only this "fairy tale" symbolizes what will really happen. Here is his story.

The Woman Babylon
rules the world like a queen.
People love her because she
promises them riches.
She tells them to forget
God, to lie and cheat
and adore her idols.

The Woman Zion has twelve children. She teaches them to love God and pray to him. At first, they are a happy family. They love each other and like to play together.

As they grow older, Zion's children stop praying. They run away and join Queen Babylon's children. Soon they start to adore idols just as others do.

A long time passes. Zion's children have scattered around the world among other people. They can't find their way home anymore. They wish they hadn't run away.

Zion prays that God will return her children. He promises to bring them back to her. He wants them to build a beautiful city for when Jesus, his beloved Son, comes.

People in the world have turned so wicked that darkness covers the earth. Out of this darkness appears a Dragon. He wants God's power, but to do evil instead of good.

The Dragon tricks people into making him their king. But after he becomes king, he forces them to obey him. His soldiers are cruel to the people who love God.

Zion and the people who love God pray for him to save them from the Dragon. God tells Zion she will have a son who will deliver her and her other children.

Zion gives birth to a boy—David—who grows up quickly. God makes him his servant. He tells David to go and find his brothers and sisters who got lost.

The people who love God love David too. He is like a light in their darkness. He teaches them the truth and exposes the lies of Queen Babylon and her children.

Queen Babylon and her children hate David. They bruise him badly and accuse him of things he didn't do. They do cruel things to the people who love God and David.

The Dragon wants to kill Zion. God helps her flee into the wilderness. The Dragon sends his army after her, but the earth opens and swallows the Dragon's army.

The Dragon wants to kill David too.
But God lifts him up to his throne in heaven.
He heals David's bruises and makes him
powerful over his enemies in the world.

An evil ruler, the King of Assyria, wants to conquer the whole world. So God tells David to call other servants to help find Zion's lost children and bring them back.

The new servants pray for God to protect them from the people who hate them. God makes them into powerful kings and queens, causing their enemies to fear.

The King of Assyria is cruel. People compare him to a beast. He tells them that if they don't bow down to him, they will die. But the people who love God refuse.

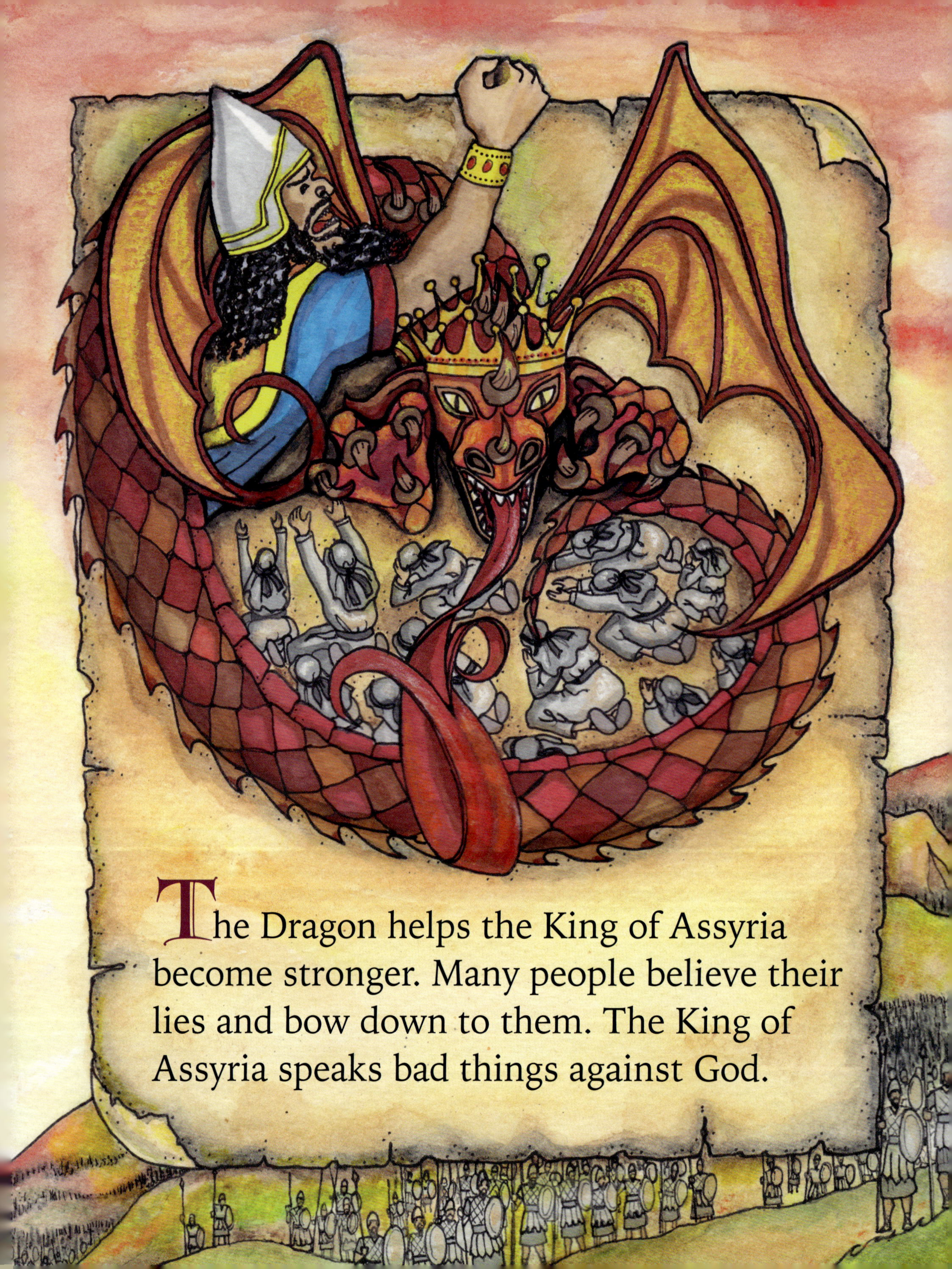

The Dragon helps the King of Assyria become stronger. Many people believe their lies and bow down to them. The King of Assyria speaks bad things against God.

The King of Assyria gathers a large army of soldiers. The kings of many nations give him their armies too. Together, they make the strongest army in the world.

The King of Assyria builds himself a palace in the sky. He wants to rule the world like a god. He commands his armies to capture all people and burn their cities.

Zion's children have started praying to God again. The righteous servants hurry to find them. Like loving fathers and mothers, they lead the children into the wilderness.

God protects Zion's children in the wilderness with a cloud of glory. They travel to where God wants them to build the city for Jesus. They help to make it beautiful.

Many people in the world die when the King of Assyria's armies burn their cities. They burn Queen Babylon and her children too—all who love and adore her idols.

The King of Assyria
wants to kill Zion too.
But David pulls him down
from the sky. The King of
Assyria rages in anger as he
falls into a deep, burning pit.

David fights the Dragon and throws him into the same burning pit with the King of Assyria. He locks the gate of the pit so they can't get out for a long time.

Zion has become young again. When Jesus comes, he will marry her. Her children bring her into the beautiful city. They adorn her with jewels for the wedding.

Everyone in the city is waiting for Jesus to come. One day, bright white clouds billow up in the morning sky. Is it Jesus? Is he coming? People excitedly tell each other about it.

The light of Jesus shines brighter than the sun as he descends in power and glory. Many angels are with him, singing and blowing trumpets.

At last he is here!

Jesus enters a beautiful palace David has built for him. Everyone is invited when he marries Zion and makes her his Queen. They praise Jesus and rejoice in him.

The world changes into Paradise. Animals play among beautiful flowers and trees. The servants rule with Jesus and David, and people come to adore Jesus, their King.